The Art of Surveillance:

For The Uniformed Patrol Officer

Ofc. R. Dixon

[1]

"EVERY SOCIETY GETS THE KIND OF
CRIMINAL IT DESERVES. WHAT IS EQUALLY
TRUE IS THAT EVERY COMMUNITY GETS
THE KIND OF LAW ENFORCEMENT IT
INSISTS ON."

- Robert Kennedy

COPYRIGHT

DISCLAIMER

It is duly noted herein that the purchaser and/or reader and/or user of this material understands that the content found herein should not in any way be construed as legal advice. It is also understood that police work is inherently dangerous and the use of any of the information or tactics in this book is strictly up to the purchaser and/or reader and/or user who does so at their own free will. Furthermore, the purchaser and/or reader and/or user of this material also agrees that the author and publisher and any of their agents associated with this material will in no way be held liable or responsible for any injuries or death that may occur as a result of utilizing the information or tactics mentioned.

FORWARD

The following information has been compiled for the active uniformed street cop that goes out there and hits it hard every shift. These are the guys and the girls that *are* making a difference whether anybody thinks they are or not. They are the patrol officers that are not in a specialty unit but still have lots of other responsibilities on their plate throughout their shifts. They are the few, pro-active patrol officers who don't care about getting wet or going hungry for a bit, who don't ride around with their windows up and aren't afraid of getting out of their cars to talk to people in order to see what's actually going on.

This book is written for the officer who wears two sets of cuffs on their belt. Not because they're "ate-up" but because they repeatedly go out on several subjects at once. The material in this book is directed towards the officer who has a true wanton desire to do more than just collect a pay check every two weeks. If you find yourself driving around thinking there's more to being a good cop than just taking dictation from angry, condescending people, arresting drunks and writing speeding tickets, then this book is for you.

There are many special tactics in this book in which you can use immediately. The faster you apply them, the faster your felony arrests will begin to rise. The faster your felony arrests rise, the faster your misdemeanor arrests rise. That's the beauty of these operations; watching your entire arrests rise automatically once you consistently start banging out those felony arrests. That's the way it works.

[5]

For example, say you arrest somebody with a couple rocks of cocaine, a felony, and what do they always have on them? A stem, right? There's your misdemeanor. If somebody runs from you, that's another misdemeanor. It's very tidy how it all works out. Now, by arrests I'm talking about solid arrests such as possession of rock cocaine, carrying concealed weapons and tampering with evidence just to name a few. 'Crumbing' (the act of arresting someone for being in possession of just a miniscule amount of dope) a bad guy is a pretty shitty thing to do to someone. But, and I repeat, BUT, if you have to you have to… and by all means do so. There's a ton of legitimate reasons why you might have to crumb someone. Just don't make those the only arrests you make. Cutting people breaks is a tactic upon itself and can be very beneficial to you and your partner later on down the road. Cutting people some slack will raise your 'street-cred' and gain you some respect out there; respect and credibility that you will definitely need and come to appreciate.

As your arrests continue to go up your knowledge and experience will continue to grow as well and you'll need every ounce of that knowledge and experience later on when these cases finally make it to court. If you stay on this track, pretty soon other officers will start coming up to you congratulating you on your arrests and then not just your supervisor, but many supervisors will start to take notice of your hard work. From there, the possibilities are endless. BUT! While you're still the FNG on the squad, remember, it takes a lot of time to build that kind of trust and camaraderie with senior officers and supervisors. We don't just trust our lives to anyone, you know? And expect to get a lot of good-hearted crap thrown your way for being so proactive in your endeavors as well. That's basically the only way you'll know that another cop appreciates you or not. And, as well, since we don't live in La-La Land, there will be the officers that will just plain talk shit about you for being so proactive but just keep in mind, that has nothing to do with you, that's all their issues at play.

So by applying the tactics in this book, you'll be well on your way to proving to your Department that you're worthy, level-headed and most importantly, squared-away. Your legacy is in your hands. You can squeak by on patrol by doing the bare bones minimum then go hide in CID or you can take the initiative and make things happen. As you'll see in the chapters to come, the latter approach usually throws the bad guys off so much that it, more often than not, shuts everything down for the night leaving you in control of your zone and not them. Remember, when you're dealing with element of street crime and the thug-mentality, you have to be proactive as opposed to reactive. Proactive yields power. Reactive yields headaches and all you'll be doing are chasing the bad guys after they've robbed someone or shot someone or pistol-whipped somebody senseless. Be proactive early and stop the madness before your only option is to become reactive.

INTRODUCTION/BACKGROUND

I've learned a lot in the past 15+ years about law enforcement and human nature. A lot of it I'd like to forget but there's been some really, really good times as well. And like everyone else, I had to start somewhere. So I started in a place that was familiar for me; a ten mile long luxury resort island. I knew two of the sergeants really well and used to do ride-a-longs on the island all the time. Already having the police bug from my grandfather who was a city cop in Pittsburgh, along with numerous other family members, I naturally enough put myself through the academy and got hired on where my buddies worked. After securing Officer of the Year my rookie year and the year after that, I began to realize something. Something was missing. And then it dawned on me. CRIME! There was no real crime on the island! Sure there were burglaries but nothing ever in progress. This was a place where everything was gated and nobody was home six months out of the year. So when you got a call that it 'occurred past' we're talking it was probably months ago before it was discovered. Needless to say, the only thing I wanted to do was to get out of there and fight real crime. I did learn the basics out there and I'm very thankful for my time on 'the rock' as we called it but by my third year out there I knew it was definitely time to move on.

After a very drawn-out hiring process, I left the island life for the hood and I have to tell you, I was in heaven! I went from a 20 officer department to a 200 officer department and I loved every second of it. During my first phase of field training, my FTO and I, myself at the wheel, got into a huge pursuit that ended with a spectacular crash when the bad guy clipped a cement light pole and flipped his vehicle right smack in the middle of some projects. Without a scratch on us or my FTO's patrol car, we took the bad guy into custody, kept the ridiculously hostile crowd back, all while gathering 23 pounds of marijuana and a butt load of cash. From that instant on I was hooked. The rush from that chase was like no other. Far from the comforts and security of amusement parks, however, this was a thrill ride with the distinct possibility of death involved and I loved it.

That honeymoon stage of my law enforcement career actually lasted for quite some time. For the first five years I had nothing but love for the job and loved doing my job. But initially, after getting out of field training and getting out on my own, I got to know the guys on my shift and I started to see how the different districts where I did my patrols operated. Sadly enough, it didn't take me long to discover which officers in those districts and zones worked and didn't work. Whether that was due to fear or laziness or a little of both remained to be seen. You could tell a lot about an officer just by the district they wanted to work in. The city I work for is broken up in to three districts; North, Central and South. If you bid to work the North side, you were in the shit. It was the hood, make no mistake about it and you were busy. North side's got all the characteristics of South Central, L.A., just a lot smaller. It has it all: dope, guns, drive-bys, AK's, rusty revolvers, stolen cars, rock rentals, domestics, robberies, pitbulls, projects, stolen cable, shot houses and absolutely no code enforcement whatsoever. That being said, however, there are a lot of very nice, pro-police, good people on the North side as well but you just never see them or hear from them because they're afraid, they keep to themselves and they'd rather not get involve. They are people that are just getting by themselves and don't wish to get caught up in any extra drama.

The Central District is downtown for the most part; all high-rise condos on the water and businesses. Central's claim to fame is the inordinate amount of transients that have flocked here in droves ever since the City approved the building of one of the largest Salvation Army's on the East Coast. There's more than enough social services here for homeless people but these transients are vagrants and these vagrants in particular want nothing except to drink, smoke spice and to have everything given to them. This includes three or four free meals a day, free clothing, free shoes, free bedding, free chairs, you name it they want it available to them so they can spend their money on the things that matter; getting drunk and getting high. Talk about having a sense of entitlement... these transients/vagrants here have rewritten the book on it. The real fun happens downtown when the vagrants clash with the business owners; never a dull moment. Besides those issues, the Central District will keep you somewhat busy but it dies off after 2:00am when the bars close.

We are now left with the South District. The South District is very snooty; mostly all residential with half of it being million and multi-million dollar homes on or near the water. The South District has its' share of domestics and does get in-progress burglaries but as far as the night goes… it stays pretty quiet.

So, by seeing where each officer bid to work, you got a pretty good idea of their work ethic. North side officers were always the go-getters, way active and loved to chase. Central cops liked to get into the mix of things but were a little bit more reserved and South side cops were either considered lazy or worse yet, 'scared' to work up north. Albeit, we did have staggered shifts with each district starting 45 minutes after the last so scheduling conflicts could be resolved by working South and let me just clarify this, not every officer that worked South side was lazy or scared. It was, however, a known hiding place. Enough said about that.

I got very lucky, however, and had a stud for a sergeant when I started on our north side. Our sergeant let us play hard and backed us 100%. But we never took advantage of that. With all sincerity, that sergeant still is and will forever be, just plain awesome. I've been through a few more sergeants and a lot of different units since but for the purposes of this book, I want to stick with and focus on the uniformed patrol officer because that is where everyone starts out and that's the first place you'll have the chance to shine. Using the tools and tactics in this book will definitely give you an edge. An edge you'll need to advance you in your law enforcement career.

One thing you'll have to realize, especially in law enforcement, is that change is inevitable. There's always new case law coming out and revisions to ordinances. And as soon as an officer does something off the wall and gets busted for it you can bet there will be a change in your G.O.'s and S.O.P.'s. But some things come unexpectedly and take the wind right out of your sails. Pretty much out of the blue, our Chief changed our very liberal pursuit policy to read that we could only chase forcible felon type stuff. It goes without saying but that really rusted up our wheels. We were devastated and pissed off. Hell, our forte was stolen cars, dope and guns; the trifecta of arrests. My awesome partner and I initiated twenty-some documented car pursuits in the last 12 months prior to the change ourselves. That's not to mention all the undocumented ones and ones where we were the second, third fourth or the twelfth car "paralleling" the pursuit. Needless to say we were pretty crushed by the Chief's decision. We looked like complete idiots to the bad guys. Imagine the two of us standing eight feet away from each other watching the car we just pulled speed off from between us. The only thing left to do after that happens is to walk calmly back to the car, turn off the blues, go 10-8, then beat the shit out of the inside of the car.

Everything happens for a reason however and I must admit though, the new policy did make us branch out and become more diverse. If it wasn't for the new policy, we might have never got out of our cars in the first place. Not that we didn't watch the corners before but that was the start of us getting into surveillance mode. This is when we started perfecting our surveillance techniques and this is when we started making surveillance into art.

So we went back to watching the corners and started going after the street level dealers as opposed to going after the vehicles that just purchased. We'd see the same faces on the same corners every night. So we started watching them and we started popping them. Instead of chasing bad guys in vehicles, we started chasing bad guys on foot. We had plans devised and utilized them as much as we could. But it wasn't as easy as all of that. Popping dopers takes some skills. You can't just roll up, jump out and expect them to tell you where they're hiding their dope. This book will teach you those skills so you don't look like a fool out on the street.

The following chapters cover the art of urban surveillance while in uniform, on patrol, and in a marked unit. I call it an art because you have to get your own style down and create a method that works for you and your partner and zone partners. I also call it an art because any cop in a specialty unit wearing black BDU's driving an unmarked car should be able to watch and pop dope dealers. It's when you're in full uniform, in a marked unit and having to listen to the radio every second that requires skills. I cover what's important: the best times to conduct surveillance, the different techniques involved, the quickest ways to get in and out, get set up, how not to get burnt and what to do if you do get burnt. At the completion of this book, you'll have the knowledge needed to make excellent felony arrests all night long that will not only make you and your squad look high and tight but will give you the knowledge and experience that's vital to succeed in the courtroom. A lot of officers forget that there's always two parts to an arrest: what happens in the street and what happens in depos and in court. If you can get to the point where you're thinking about depos and court before you make the arrest, even if it's just ever so briefly, it's going to make things a whole lot easier. Remember what Denzel Washington's character said in Training Day. "In order to protect the sheep you have to catch the wolf. And it takes a wolf to catch a wolf." If you can think like a defense attorney and do the things during the arrest that he or she is inevitably going to ask, that's half the battle right there. Being a top notch police officer means that you have to be able to physically fight the bad guys on the streets and then mentally fight their well-paid defense attorneys in depos and in court.

Thank you for taking the time to read this book. By holding it in your hands it already says a lot about you as an officer. To me it says, you're not lazy, you're not afraid to get dirty, and you love putting bullies in their place. I hope you can take some of this knowledge with you to work every night. I know Patrol is a highly reactive place to be, but when the opportunity arises, take advantage of it. Have some fun. Make some memories. There's a whole different world going on outside the security of the old black and whites. People see us coming from blocks away in our marked units; we're like the ice cream man driving down the street. But if you hide your car and take time to look and listen, I promise you'll be both enlightened and at times disgusted by the human behavior you observe. How could you pass up an opportunity to partake in that? As Chapter 5 talks about, you might even be inclined to video tape some of these knuckleheads!

Chapter 1

Surveillance Objectives - Pros vs. Cons

Prior to embarking on most endeavors, it is wise to weigh both the pros and the cons of the any given situation. Getting in to position and doing surveillance is no exception. For the purposes of this book, if you'd like to start upping your felony arrests sooner than later, the pros of initiating a surveillance session far outweigh the cons as you shall see. As we begin to discuss what it takes the uniformed patrol officer to initiate a successful surveillance operation, we find that many factors affect our every move. That being said, the biggest and basic pros of doing surveillance are: 1) It quickly gets you familiar with the players/bad-guys/dopers in your zone 2) It's an excellent opportunity to show your supervisors you can organize a small group of guys 3) It makes you think outside of the box 4) It gets you out of the car and breaks up the monotony of your shift, especially if you're working 12's and 5) If done right, it will significantly up your felony and misdemeanor arrests as mentioned above.

The cons of doing surveillance are few and most times unavoidable. The biggest one is probably the saddest one in that you'll need to find others willing to do surveillance with you. Along with that there will be a lot of different reasons why this is true. A few examples would be that your department simply does not have the man-power, your Sergeant doesn't want you off 'playing' or you might just have a lazy squad. Other cons are that it's much harder to get into a position of observance without the cover of darkness. (Remember, this information is geared for the uniformed patrol officer, one of the most recognizable figures on the face of the earth. Anybody in plain clothes can slip in anywhere, anytime. If you can't, you got issues!) Handling your calls for service is always a problem as well because you want to get out there and watch what's going on when it's going on, but you can't just blow your zone off either. While you're assigned to Patrol, remember this, calls for service override everything else. They might all be BS calls but it doesn't matter, they are your BS calls. A great way to circumvent that, which I mention later, is to get someone willing to cover your zone while you're doing the actual surveillance. Maintaining excellent zone integrity on a regular basis becomes very important at this point. By zone integrity I mean that you take the calls that come out in your zone so the officer in the next zone over doesn't have to handle them. This is fine every once in a while, but abuse it and see how quickly how hostile things get. So take the calls in your zone. That way, when you need your zone covered to do things such as surveillance, your squad zone partners won't mind as much, especially if you help them out with whatever they need. If you're never in your zone and units are constantly getting dispatched to work your crashes and domestic disputes, people are not going to be very receptive to you. That kind of work ethic gets really old really fast. You wouldn't appreciate it very much if the officers next to you were grabbing all these awesome dope arrests while you were grinding through all the crap calls in their zone. Be part of the solution, not part of the problem. I'll elaborate further on this in the upcoming chapters as it becomes more relevant.

Obtaining Permission

There are basically two forms of permission that you're going to want to acquire. First and foremost, it's paramount that you get permission from your immediate supervisor. Not only does it let him or her know where you guys are at, it lets them know you're out being proactive and productive and not just hanging out at the Smoothie King. You guys are going to be quiet on the radio while you're getting into position so you don't want your supervisor mistaking radio silence for anything other than it is.

NO TRESPASSING OR LOITERING ON THIS PROPERTY

The next permission you should be seeking is the use of land adjacent to where the bad guys have set up shop. Most times, asking permission from a homeowner to use their garage for surveillance is like asking a dog if it would like a bone. Most times they eat it up. The only consideration here is to find out what team the homeowner is routing for. If he or she is the complainant and wants the dope dealing thugs moved on, then you're in. If the dopers are kin, forget it. One last note, although you don't need permission to get into a row of shrubs next to the sidewalk because that's generally considered in the city's right-of-way, if possible, it might be a good idea to let homeowners know that you'll be in the area. This is especially important when you're trying to avoid dogs and 10,000 watt porch lights. You'll find however, sadly enough, that the dope dealers pick the corners that offer least resistance, meaning that the surrounding neighbors most likely are not going to be as cooperative as you'd like them to be. Let's face it, the bad guys wouldn't be on that land or wouldn't run there or sell there or hide their dope there if *they* didn't already have permission from the homeowner themselves! There are a lot of homeowners out there that don't like the police so much and would be more than willing to accept a couple twenty spots or Benjamin's from the dopers to turn a blind eye. But that's okay. That's why we utilize tactics in our endeavors. And that's why the bad guys still go to jail.

Now it's not all just brimstone, fire and hate out there. More often than not, legitimate landlords call and ask the police to help. When you get that type of scenario presenting itself, it's usually game on so jump on the opportunity and take advantage of it! Usually, the homeowner or landlord is so fed up with the drug dealing that they'll give you the keys to the place and stock the fridge for you. They'll do whatever you ask of them to get rid of the dope dealers in their front yard or on their corner. Just make sure if your sergeant allows you to use someone's property, and this should go without saying, but make sure you clean up after yourselves. You don't want the homeowner to come back to what looks like the morning after the super bowl party. In fact, if the dopers are there and you know what to look for, you won't be in the house long anyways. But, more often than not, people that want dope dealers moved on usually want to remain anonymous and who can blame them? The harsh reality is that once a thug realizes a certain property is pro-police, their true colors usually come shining through in barrages of verbal assaults and intimidation tactics that include smashing out the windows in both the home and in the family car along with flattening the tires to boot. Thugs are capable of doing unimaginable damage both physical and mental. Don't ever underestimate the enemy.

A common scenario during shift briefing that incorporates the above issues would go something like the following. Your sergeant gives you a hot spot in your zone and tells you there's been an increase in the level of illegal narcotics activity and wants you and your partner to check it out. Now he or she may have just told you to check it out, but what your sergeant didn't say is that his or her lieutenant told them and the captain told the lieutenant and the chief's on the captain's ass because the complainant is an ex-commissioner who's always hated the police to begin with and all the chief wants is for it to go away nicely. Now, regardless of the complainant, you just bought it and your supervisor doesn't want to see it come up again. It's your problem now and you should probably document the things that you're going to do to combat the problem because as sure as you're reading this, if you don't, it will come back to bite you in the butt. All it takes is a few sentences to cover you. One quick way is to write up an employee observation that would get forwarded to the City's public works or streets department that requests some more lighting in the area and explain in the narrative that the place has become dangerously unsafe as a direct result of not having enough light. Explain that it has become a haven for illegal narcotics sales and you've received numerous citizen complaints in the area. If this area continues to be a problem, or if someone gets shot, or is in any way the victim of a serious crime, you're going to need to be able to show exactly what you've done to try and correct the problem. Just keep in mind, getting lighting in the area is not your main objective, it's an objective but do not get side tracked by that. Write it up and be done with it, you've got lots of other stuff to worry about.

Now, unless all you do is surf the internet for real estate bargains or automotive auctions during your shift, you should already know where the hot spots and problem areas are in your zone of responsibility without having to have your supervisor tell you that there's a problem. That includes both real and perceived problems. An example of a real problem would be dopers doing hand to hands in broad daylight. A perceived problem is when you got a group of old men that have been coming to the same park bench for fifty years to partake in a few adult beverages and somebody reports them for selling illegal drugs instead of the dopers on the outskirts of the park. You need to be able to distinguish who's on the corner and who's on the benches then be able to articulate that back to your supervisor. It's all about CYA, nothing more, nothing less.

So whether you inherit a problem area from your sergeant or decide to tackle a known problem area on your own, you'll just need to nail down a few other factors such as who the dealers are and where they're dealing from ('where' meaning are they on private or public property). Most times you will know who the players are that are dealing. Your FTO should have definitely made you aware of these problem areas and the individuals so that you can address them by yourself when you get out on your own. If you don't know who's on the corner then call someone on the radio and ask them to do a drive by to identify. Information is king. The more Intel you can gather on a target the safer everyone will be. Depending on who's working, there's a pretty good chance that someone will be able to identify the subject. Once the targets are identified, there's a lot you can establish about them right off the bat such as their prior arrest history, is he or she violent or not, does they usually carry a weapon, has he or she ever been arrested with a weapon, do they usually sell rock or weed or pills (difference between felony or misdemeanor arrest) do they have active warrants, are they on probation, is he or she a runner, where did they run to last time, where did they keep the dope last time, was it on them or hidden on the property, or are they trespassed from the area? All these questions can be answered very quickly. A lot of us keep this information stored in files in the back of our minds and are able to retrieve it instantly upon seeing dopers.

If the bad guy or girl is not known, it's still game on, just expect more of the unexpected. If they're going to be dealing dope in your zone you're going to meet them one way or the other anyway. Remember, there are a lot of different ways to play the dope game. If there's a fresh face out on the corner that you can't ID and you're Spidey senses are all over the charts and you don't have time to watch them, then get out on him or her and attempt to make a citizen contact. You'll find out real quick what they're all about. They'll either be 'tough guys' and hold their ground, slink away as you're getting out of the car or take off like a bat out of hell. A little insight on the aforementioned behavior is this: if they stick around and hold their ground, then they're not holding dope or at least the dope is not on them. If they try and slink away they most likely have a warrant or they're more than likely holding dope or have a trespass issued against them but if they beat feet and flee upon sight of you, the chances of them having a warrant, holding dope or having been previously trespassed from the area, rise significantly in your favor. If they do take off, don't give chase unless you have something concrete on them. Remember, the citizen contact was a fact finding mission. If he takes off, that's a whole lot of information for you and your partner to store in your own internal filing systems. Besides, if they didn't get busted then they'll be back and you'll know a little bit more of what to expect the next time. And don't worry; there will be a next time. There always is. Unless you can articulate that he or she was in a high crime area plagued with illegal narcotics and violence and that subject took off running upon sight of you, a uniformed patrol officer, it's ok to let it ride. If you don't have anything to charge them with right then, then you don't have anything. It's best to check with your State Attorney to see exactly when you can chase somebody if they beat feet during a mere citizen contact.

Now, as far as the property is concerned and where exactly they're dealing at, you'll need to determine if that dealing is being done on private property, public property or in public housing. A simple drive by will confirm this. If the problem is in the street and they're operating a drive-up service where vehicles stop in the road and they walk up to it to make the deal then you're golden. Most of these operate like fast food restaurants and the only thing missing is the sign that says, 'Over a Billion Sold'. You also have your choice of bad guys here as well. You can either go after the buyer, the seller or both. In instances such as these, we'll call out the vehicle that just bought and then have a chase car pull them after they get out of the area. After a few of those stops, and hopefully before the sellers run out of dope, then we'll go in and get the dealers. It's a great night when you can get at least one of both. Doing so will significantly reduce the problem quickly in the problem area, at least while you and your partners are working. Don't worry; word of mouth is alive and well.

If dopers are on private property like up in a carport area and they never leave it and the deals are being made behind closed doors, then you're most likely going to need to get C.I.'s or 'confidential informants' involved. In cases such as those, you'll be better off shooting a thorough intelligence submission over to your narc guys. At the minimum, include who's dealing, where they're dealing and what they're dealing, any tag numbers, time of day they're most busy, and who's complaining or was it your own observation. Intel submissions are another quick way to CYA. Just make sure it's a legit submission. You'll want to avoid pissing off any narcs early in your career by writing up bogus Intel just to CYA because your sergeant's on you. And by 'narcs' I mean your undercover narcotics officers not C.I.'s. Don't get too upset about having to turn the house over to the narcs either. I'm sure there are plenty of open air street level sales to tackle without you having to get too involved. You're still a winner here as the undercover narcs are usually very good about giving props to patrol for having identified the house in the first place.

If the problem is in Public Housing, in Florida, you as an officer become an agent for the government since that's who runs projects and therefore maintain your full arrest powers.   You can also trespass people without a complainant since you are acting as that agent. Most tenants of the projects know the police have a bit more authority in the projects and would rather deal out of a private residence. Problems do arise however when there are ten people living in an apartment and the legal resident has been in jail for the past six months. The housing authority, in my experience, has always been great to work with and have always has a zero tolerance policy when it comes to dope and guns on property. It might take them a little while to figure out who needs to be evicted or trespassed but they'll do it. One final mention regarding Public Housing is that everyone that is found on Public Housing property must be able to properly identify themselves. If they don't then they get taken in for obstruction. This is due to a strict 'residents only' on property clause and the Housing Authority not wanting any repeat offenders on said property. As mentioned above, any illegal gun or narcotic violations will get you the boot from Public Housing. Even fighting could get residents thrown out. It by no means stops the activity, but it's at least a tool we can use as a deterrent.

If the problem is on an empty lot or an abandoned or vacant house where they just sort of set up shop, then a little work on our part will be required. A quick look through the property appraiser's office will generally let you know who owns the property. More often than not, most of the abandoned properties will be owned by banks. If that's the case, you might as well stop there and plan on it taking at least a week to determine actual ownership. If we're lucky enough to get a good name though, we can then go from there to determine if they're aware of the problem and if they're friend or foe. If they're friendly we can help them get their property into a Trespass Enforcement Program which in my Department, allows us to run persons off the property and make arrests on their, the property owners, behalf. It's a great tool since the property owner does not have to be present at the time. If the property owner turns out to be foe, then we have something else for him or her... It's called Nuisance Abatement. This is basically code enforcement for drug houses, houses of ill repute and prostitution. This is another great tool because once a property falls under Nuisance Abatement officers have the right to check on the property and to make sure the conditions set forth by a hearing board are actually adhered to.

A quick recap on property types and permissions is this: If dealers are selling from inside, forward the information on. If they're outside on the corner they're all yours. If they start on public and run to private, you're still golden thanks to a little term known as 'fresh-pursuit' (check your own GO's, SOP's and State Statutes. Some allow fresh pursuit only if a felony is involved which in most cases leaves marijuana (under 20 grams in Florida) out. If you're in Public Housing, use the tools you have available to you. Trespass files, requesting identification, and warrants checks. There are some tools still left out there for us to use, you just have to be aware of them.

Timing Is Everything

Timing is pretty critical during a surveillance operation as well. It will always seem that while you're on your way to a three car crash, everyone and their brother will be out selling dope. Right? Now the flip side to that is, as soon as you clear and get ready to go in, it inevitably becomes a ghost town out there. The main thing to remember about timing is that you can't expect to get out of your car just as soon as you get signed on. Shift change is usually the busiest time for officers and you can't expect your squad to handle all their calls plus yours. That's just not going to work. The best time to go is when there are no calls holding, you already ate, you're caught up on all your reports, and it's dark out. If you don't have those prerequisites then you're going to be rushing and it won't be fun it will be too stressful and too much like work. Remember, done right, surveillance and the subsequent arrests that follow is the stuff that becomes legendary amongst you and your squad mates. These are the fun times, the good times. Enjoy them and make the most of them!

CHAPTER 2

Acquiring Your Target

Merriam-Webster defines surveillance as "The observation of subjects from a position of advantage so the subjects are left unaware they are being observed." That being said, there are three objectives we must consider before playtime commences: 1) Identify who the sellers are. 2) Where can they be watched from most effectively? And 3) How to get to that point and still remain undetected.

As mentioned in Chapter 1, there are a lot of reasons why you'll want to identify your targets; officer safety being paramount. A little planning goes a long way as well. In order for your surveillance operation to be successful, you'll have to be able to get in to the area and get right back out as quickly as possible to avoid burning yourselves or the surveillance spot, especially if it's a good one. Points to consider are these: Are you going to have to literally run to a spot or do you think you can sneak in using a stealth approach? Will you have to use a diversion? Diversions are great for getting you out once arrests go down, but as you'll see in Chapter 3, if done right, diversions can also help get you in to a place as well.

To further ensure your surveillance session's success, you're going to need people to observe! That should go without saying but trust me there have been plenty of times when my squad was all pumped up to do surveillance and nobody was out. Once you do find that favorite corner, either yours or theirs, and there are people out, do not make the mistake of repeatedly driving by just to be sure they haven't left. If you drive by a second time, there won't be a need for a third. All you have to do is drive by once and act totally uninterested. Act like your talking on your phone or stuffing subpoenas into your visor. You want to be joking with your partner and act like they don't even exist. But, at the same time, you still want to try and see who it is that's out there, how many, and if they're known dealers or not. You also want to look for those very slight, furtive moves that are going to tell you who are holding the dope. Another little clue to pick up on is, as you're driving by them, watch their eyes. If one suddenly gets the deer in the headlight look, or unconsciously pulls his pants up, chances are pretty good that he's actually holding the dope. Others, if they're dirty, will take a quick glance towards their intended escape route just to make sure it's still clear. A lot of times, if you have a group of five kids selling dope, they'll already have an exit strategy in place if the cops roll up on them. It might be, if one runs they all run. Two cops chasing five kids with only one holding dope is pretty good odds for them. Another strategy will be just to hold their ground, knowing and hoping that the dope is hidden well enough that the cops won't find it. At that point, if one of them gets nervous and runs, you can bet he gets his ass beat by the others regardless of the outcome. Selling dope is serious business and they make serious money and the consequences for jeopardizing that are serious as well.

If none of the dopers appear to be overly concerned, that's a sign they're hiding the dope close by where they can get to it to make a quick sale as opposed to holding the

dope on their person. If you don't think they're holding dope on your first drive-by but you know the guys and they've been popped before for selling, set up on them. It won't take but five or ten minutes before either of two things happen: 1) It's busy out so he's going back and forth to the dope or 2) It's slow so he feels compelled to check the dope to make sure it's still there.

Now once you're sure you want to get out and watch these guys, make sure the other units in the area don't drive by either. Believe me, there's always that one numbskull officer who avoids the hood like the plague but just as sure as you're reading this, as soon as you get out the car and into position, they'll come cruising by and jack everything up; every department has one. Now, there will be a time when you'll want a marked unit to drive by as it mentions in Chapter 4 so you can see who gets nervous, who throws what down, who's holding, or where the dopes being hid, but that's your call and after you're already into position.

A short mention here on choosing your location. Most jurisdictions have enhanced penalties for selling controlled substances within 1000' of a day care, a school, or church. Look around, there are daycare's, schools and churches everywhere. Judges and juries get offended very easily at this kind of behavior versus just selling dope on any old corner. If you're going through all the work to really get these guys, you might as well give yourselves the satisfaction of sticking it to them with enhanced penalties to boot. Enhanced penalties equal higher bonds and more jail time. If you do end up being able to collar someone within the 1000 foot rule, make sure you have a traffic guy or someone with a laser shoot from where your guy was selling to the actual building that enhances the charge. Then note that exact footage, the officer's name, the type of laser and the laser's serial number all in your probable cause affidavit. Just remember a judge and jury will find it a lot harder to dismiss or minimize a case where the bad guy is selling dope near one of those enhanced buildings.

CHAPTER 3

Getting Into Position

Bad guys are so used to associating cops with patrol cars that they totally forget about officers appearing in any other mode. Their eyes are going to be peeled about to the streets, so much so that they forget about what bushes or roof tops might hold. My old partner Ronnie and I have had people pass within two feet in front of us, beside us, under

us, and over us. The key is getting out of your car quickly and swiftly. The problem is where to put your patrol car. It's got to be close enough in case you get a priority call but at the same time, it's got to be safe enough so no one knifes your tires. Before you ditch your car though, figure out from where you're going to be doing your actual surveillance. Look for thick hedges, dark shadowy areas, fence lines. Look for any roof that is accessible or for any

large trees as well. One of the most important aspects to remember here is that your background needs to be black. If you got that, you're golden. You can move around uninhibited with a black background but if you don't have it, forget it. Find somewhere else. Even if you get into position undetected, if you have to leave in a hurry you'll burn that spot. Once you burn a spot, the dopers get a little bit smarter and it ultimately makes your job a lot harder to watch them in the future. As I alluded to earlier, the great thing about doing surveillance on dopers is that they only look for one thing: police cars, marked or unmarked it doesn't matter. They can spot them from a mile away. To exploit this advantage all we have to do is mix things up a bit.

Once you've identified your targets, you'll need to decide where you're going to hide and what you're going to do with your car. There are several options here like finding a vacant house for sale then acting as if you got an alarm there then disappear into the night or park at a closed business and do the same. If you can walk in, great, if you can't, it's time for Plan B. Just remember, as soon as you step out of your car you're like Linus without his blanket and as soon as you step off the street every dog in the neighborhood will start barking. There's nothing worse than spending a half hour walking in the shadows and remaining completely stealth all the way up to that last moment when you're just about to get into position and somebody yells, "Five-O!" (Not that that's not happened to my partner and I or anything!) It happens, okay? And it sucks big time, but it does happen. Patience is your friend here. You'll find that it's sometimes a lot harder than it looks to get into position. Sometimes the planets cooperate, sometimes they don't.

Getting Dropped Off... aka: Plan B

A quicker way to get into position is to be dropped off by a neighboring zone car or if your sergeant's willing, by him or her. Most times you won't want to bother your sergeant but if they need a break and they got some time, then by all means use them. Just don't ever put their name on any paperwork that might result in them going to a depo or court. That would not be good. Sergeants are great for help out in the street but dragging them into court with you over a possession and obstruction charge is a definite no-no.

Getting dropped off works well because it allows you to park further away like at a substation where your vehicle will be much safer. On the flip side to that however, you'll need to be picked up as well. That can suck if a high priority call comes out and everybody leaves you guys to thumb your way back.

Once dropped off, you'll still need to weave your way through houses and yards to your preplanned target location. To get there undetected, you're going to have to wear either your rain jacket turned to the black side or a black BDU shirt over your patrol shirt. Your patrol shirt is way too flashy not to be covered. The darker you are the better. Remember: to catch a criminal you have to think like a criminal. When's the last time you saw a burglar wearing any bling? That's just what your collar brass and badge is… bling. And they'll reflect light off of a street light in a heartbeat.

Creating a Diversion

Creating a diversion to get you into to your preplanned target area is sheer genius and works like 99% of the time. If it doesn't, it's definitely operator error. How this works is that you get at least three marked units and you have them scream up to an area just shy of your target location with lights and sirens chirping. You want to be close enough to get the people in the areas attention but still far enough away so they know for a fact that they are not the object of that attention. By doing this, you can bet all eyes will be peeled on those marked units but they won't be able to tell specifically what's happening.

Now, the beauty of this tactic is that the two of you that are going to be doing the actual surveillance are going to be hiding in the rear of one of the patrol cars. This requires that you don't shut the doors so you can get out. Now you guys jump out with everyone else but as the other officers are making a scene and creating the actual diversion, you guys slink off out into the darkness. As soon as you're clear from the scene and sure you have not been detected, simply contact your diversion team and have them clear out. It's just that easy and like I said, it works just about every time.

We did that very same diversion at 18th Street and Central Ave in our city but the only difference was is that we rolled right up onto the same corner where the drug activity was taking place. We knew however, that he would return once we left because of a few things. 1) He was not that bright, 2) he lived right there on the corner, 3) he kept a little rock on him, just enough for a few sales or one nice sale, and the rest he kept in the house on private property, and 4) he always ran into his house if the cops were on to him. So like I said, we did just that. I was hiding in the back of a marked unit with my rain coat on. We flew up to the corner, lights on, the whole nine yards, did a bunch of yelling and screaming and as that was going on, I snuck out of the back of the car and immediately climbed a huge oak tree that was right on the corner. It was beautiful. As soon as I was up and out of sight, I gave the all clear and everyone took off just as fast as we showed up.

It wasn't five minutes later that that knuckle head came right back out to the corner. In less than15 minutes I had three documented sales less than 15 feet away from me. Several times I could have jumped right down on his head. He never looked up once, never. Now, that's not to say it went perfectly according to plan. But we did affect the arrest and had a possession of rock cocaine, tampering with evidence and an obstruction without violence charge in the books. That's two felonies and a misdemeanor. The best part about that particular arrest was that it put this particular individual way over in points and off to prison he went for 22 months.

CHAPTER 4

Counter Surveillance

Who's Watching You While You're Watching Them

While you're driving through a documented high crime area and you hear the phrase, "Five-O!" or "Fire in the Hole!" yelled out, it's not just somebody trying to be cute. It's an early warning device used to make people aware of what's going on whilst illegal activity takes place. In all actuality it's more like a last ditch effort to warn someone because by the time that's barked out, we're right there anyways. It really is a very sad commentary on the community as a whole when there's that much illegal activities going on that random people feel the need to call out the police every time we roll around a corner.

But not just random people call out the police. The dopers on the corner pay to have spotters warn them of approaching units and dopers don't care who they employ. So, now those little kids riding around on bikes become not so innocent. Not that they're accomplices or anything because pretty much all they know is that they get a couple bucks every time they call out a squad. They do learn from there, however, and for many, it's the catalyst that got them in to the dope game. By the time they reach into the teens, making easy money already has a firm grip on their psyche. In a society where you can make more in one day on the street than you can working all week at a burger joint, the decision becomes not that tough to make. Crack heads are used in just the same way, however, instead of getting a little cash, they work for rock or for crumbs of rock I should say.

When Nextel's came out all you heard was the chirping of the alert when you drove through the hood. "Beep-beep. Five-O two streets over." "Beep-beep. They gettin' out the car." Everyone had one. We can't say much though. We operated from Nextel's a lot back then as well. Only when we had to did we get on the police radio and by then everything was already neatly coordinated and we were in a full blown pursuit. It got so bad at one point that our sergeant scribbled out the word 'Nextel's' on a piece of paper, taped it to a trash can and had it sitting beside him on top of the table where he conducted his briefings from. Upon entering the room, we voluntarily threw them in the trash and then had to promise that we'd use the car radio. We did get our phones back after briefing and still laugh 'til this day about that. It was so funny because he couldn't figure out how we all just happen to be in the 'right place at the right time, EVERYTIME!' Until, that is, when my partner and I were standing with him one night up on the block and one of our Nextel's went off. All you could hear was one of our zone partners screaming, "Okay! East bound on 29th approaching 301! Where the fuck are you guys!?" We all looked at each other and in that instant he knew exactly what we had been up to. He was cool about it, though. We just sort of looked at each other then looked at him until he yelled at us to go join the pursuit. As calm as could be the next thing you'd hear on the police radio was, "3203 dispatch... We're behind a white Monte Carlo northbound on 301 from 29th, Florida tag yada, yada, yada, could we get another unit please?"

Enough story time. The main thing to remember when conducting surveillance is that whether it looks like it or not, there are always going to be people watching you. The trick then becomes to arrive at your prearranged location undetected. Use what you know to your advantage. If you're doing an operation during the day, do it when most kids are in school as opposed to a Saturday afternoon. If you're doing it at night, do it when most kids should be in for the night. I know that's a joke but, you get the idea.

CHAPTER 5

The Watching Bad Guys

Finally, You're In Position

Now that you've made it this far and the stars and planets have all aligned perfectly allowing you and your partner to watch someone or a group of people, one of the most important things to do now is to keep your officers,

your take down team in particular, update on what's happening. Even if there's nothing going on at the moment, let them know there's nothing going on and keep in mind, however exciting it was for you to get into position, your take down team has just been sitting around that whole time. Knowing how active cops are, it's hard for go-getters to just sit in one place for any length of time. If you let your team get bored, they will stray. Case in point: when my squad created that diversion to get me into that oak tree on 18th Street. The kid I was watching was having some luck selling but it wasn't going very fast. I also wanted to observe three sales from this particular individual so come court time it would be a bit more solid. As soon as he made his last sale, I called in the team. Then I called in the team again. Then I checked my radio; everything good there. I kept calling and still nothing. Mind you, I couldn't yell into the radio because I was literally just ten feet above this guy and about thirty feet away. When I switched over to our main channel two of the guys went to back someone up nearby and the third, my sergeant, was on 10-50, a traffic stop. Needless to say I had a few choice words for all of them. Everything worked out but it had the propensity to go south very quickly. I didn't want to burn the tree and I really didn't want to just jump down on his head. If things are slow, people get bored and tend to want to start doing their own thing. That is understandable; however, never intentionally leave anyone out by themselves. There's a lot going on and a lot of commotion that surrounds a take down. It always drawls a crowd when a couple of cars come screeching up with several cops running out of them. More times than not, a short foot pursuit ensues as well.

Keep in my mind also that the above arrest itself, after the take down team finally got there, made enough of a commotion for me to be able to get out of that tree undetected. Most times, however, the guys and girls doing

[43]

the surveillance will a way out without being detected as discussed in chapter 3.

If Nobody's Selling... Nobody's Selling

As you get into position and things begin to settle down for you, the area should return to business as usual pretty quickly. Keep in mind however; if you've gotten in undetected then there should be no reason why things should be anything less than business as usual. At this point, you'll be able to see exactly what's going on: who's selling, where the most likely place is the dope is being hid, if it's on them or hid nearby.

If you don't see any of those things happening, you're going to have to make a decision. Do you wait and hope the dope returns or do you call it? There are a lot of factors to consider when making the decision and you always have to keep in mind that resources will more than likely be stretched thin when you're doing these types of operations. Other considerations will likely be if you know the seller or not, if you're not pressed for time, who else is in the area with the suspected seller and how much traffic is in the area; including foot, bicycle and vehicle.

There's no shame in your game when calling an operation off. That's just the way it goes. You either need to find a different area or just get back in the car and handle calls. You'll find that your squad mates will be a lot more likely to help you with your surveillance effort in the future if you don't hold them up for very long. But again, as sure as you're reading this right now, if you keep them away from stuff that they want to do in hopes that something might turn up and you've already been sitting on a place for 45 minutes, you can bet they won't be so eager to help next go 'round. Don't worry; they'll be plenty of opportunities for you to get into surveillance mode.

Remember; just because the effort itself may not have panned-out this time, that doesn't mean that you just come tromping out behind cover all pissed-off and yelling. That will absolutely kill any chances of surveillance on that spot in the future. Regardless of how big of a fail it was, you still must back out of your spot and remain undetected.

If They Are Selling

We just touched on what to do if the peeps you're watching are not selling. Now for the fun stuff; what are your responsibilities after you get into position and you observe that the bad guys actually are selling? First things first, those doing the actual surveillance are going to be those that get subpoenaed to go to court without a doubt. So, in order for you to successfully prosecute your case, you're going to have to be very specific on your probable cause affidavit. So first of all you'll need to identify the dope. The use of binoculars is definitely recommended. You're going to have to be able to articulate what the bad guy was selling. Was it pills, weed, rock, some designer drug?

After you got a grip on what is being sold, you're going to need to identify who the seller is. Is he a known individual? And then give out the description of the seller. Be as descriptive as you can to include race, sex, approximate age, clothing; ball caps, shirts, pants, colors being flown if any; facial hair if any; sunglasses, regular glasses; sneakers and type of shoes in general, high-tops, low-tops, slides; complexions, white, light skin, dark skin; type of hair, straight, short, long, twisties, dreds, plats, etc. Not only are you making mental notes of all these points but, if at all possible, making physical notes as well is a great idea. And do not forget the importance of communication. You will need to have clear communication to your team of who is selling and what he or she is selling. You're going to probably be pretty close to the bad guys if you're outdoors under a bush or something so you'll need to talk into your radio loud enough so your team hears but not so loud that those you're watching obviously hear you. And while we're on the subject of communication, make sure your radio is surveillance ready. Meaning that your radio doesn't beep every time you key up or that your radio's display doesn't light up and give your position way. A fat piece of black duct tape works well for the second issue.

On a side note, in reference to the clothing being worn on any particular night, don't ever underestimate the street smarts that a lot of these individuals have. A lot of them out there selling will be wearing their own 'uniform of the day' as we called it. Whether that consists of red shirts with black shorts or white wife-beaters with tan cargo shorts, whatever they decide to wear, they'll all be wearing the same thing. Think about it. What do most cops blurt out upon the sight of somebody running from them? Race, shirt color, pants color and direction of travel. Now the problem is you got four or five guys all running in the same direction and all wearing the same exact thing. Hopefully your take down team will be good enough to get them all stopped, and again, it's going to be up to the surveillance team to positively identify the actual sellers and where the dope is.

Now that you've communicated to your team and updated them on who is holding and what they're holding, you'll now need to determine where the dope is being held. If they are not keeping the dope on them then it will be close by. By simply watching them exclusively you'll be able to identify exactly where the dope is. If the dope is being held on them, they will continually check it to make sure it is still there. Even though they just checked it and felt that it was in the left rear pocket, psychologically, they check it over and over without even realizing they're doing it. On a side note, if someone is carrying a gun they'll do the same exact thing, they just cannot leave it alone. Same goes with it if they're keeping it in, let's say a mailbox. They'll open and close the mailbox repeatedly just to make sure it hasn't evaporated on them. Sometimes, however, it will be a bit more difficult to pin point where the dope is but all your doubts will be eased once a buyer comes in to the picture. And if the difficult one that you couldn't make out leaves when a buyer approaches, enters a structure and then returns, then you know it's being kept in the structure.

Places Where People Hide Dope

Some more common hiding places are palm trees, or any trees or shrubs, in the tops of pipes sticking out of the ground or fence caps. Anything on the ground that has a lid will be used, like a water meter box and if they're up on a porch or something then barbecue grills are always a good bet as well as in mailboxes. Gas tanks on vehicles, inside the fuel door. M&M tubes and candy lip stick containers are very common and can be slide down the crack of the ass relying on the fact that most cops won't go 'that far' with the search. If you are a thorough searcher, which you should be anyways, you can bet the bank that as soon as you get close to the dope they'll start yelling and screaming everything from harassment to sexual battery, anything to deflect the fact their hiding dope on them. And as sure as you're reading this right now, the second you entertain that bullshit the next second you'll be in an all-out foot pursuit. Know what you can do and what you can't do before you're dealing with the dopers in the streets. Can you pull someone's boxers away from their body to see if they're hiding dope after you've been conducting surveillance on them? Yes you can. If you're not sure, ask a supervisor prior to you going out and getting into position or call a supervisor to the scene if you are detaining an uncooperative subject and you haven't found the dope yet.

Chances are, if they run and you end up hooking them up just for the obstruction charge when you catch them, and you will catch them, then the jail will eventually find anything hidden where you wouldn't want to go anyways. How will you know if the jail found something? Believe me, dispatchers love calling you out on that kind of stuff. They can't just say, "3203, please call booking reference your last arrest." Oh no, it's more like: "3203, booking called and wants you back 51 to them. They found a quantity of cocaine and marijuana on the 10-15 you just brought in and wants you to return." The jail shouldn't get too worked up about that kind of stuff as long as it's not a weapon of any kind. Finding weapons on people at the jail is a whole new ballgame, a very real, scary, and dangerous ballgame. Especially after realizing you just transported this person that was sitting behind you for however many blocks and he or she had a freaking gun on them the whole time or a knife that they were getting ready to shank you with as soon as you helped them out of the backseat. The bottom line is this, search your prisoners well. Everybody listens to the radio. If you keep getting called back to the jail, there's a problem and it usually comes down to one of the following three instances. Either you're not explaining to your arrestee the fact that anything brought into the jail becomes 'Introduction of Contraband' (which becomes a nice felony charge) or your arrestee believes that they can hide the dope successfully or your searching techniques need improvement.

[49]

CHAPTER 6

When You've Seen Enough

Determining Who to Go After – The Seller Or The Buyer

During your surveillance effort, in a perfect world, you would have enough people to both jump out and grab the seller and you would have a chase car available to pull the buyers. Most of the time it's either one or the other but there is a way to make arrests of both parties and is really a great option.

If your team was to just target one or the other, the seller or the buyer, then there would be a piece missing when it comes time for court. If you get the seller, you're hoping that he has dope on him so you can make the arrest. No dope, no arrest. If you get the buyer, you're hoping you can find the dope he just purchased but again, no dope, no arrest. The way we tied everything together with a nice little bow was to watch the bad guy do at least three sales before we pulled the plug on him or her. After each sale we would have our take down car(s) that were out of the immediate area, go after the buyers. That way we would have the dope, we would know exactly what they were selling and for how much and we would have the possession arrest and a vehicle seizure if we wanted it. Most importantly we would know if the seller was actually selling the real deal or just selling 'dreams', fake rock or weed made to look like the real deal. The ends of crisp fast-food French fries seemed to be a favorite to use. You could make a case for someone selling dreams but the State Attorney usually declines to prosecute. That's not to say, however, that there wouldn't be an obstruction charge still in there somewhere.

So now that you got your take down team going after the buyers, the seller is still feeling pretty good. He's making money and everything is great. Keep in mind when you're communicating with the take down team about the buyers, you have to give out as much information as you can. Are they in a car, on foot, on a bicycle? Which direction is he or she headed? If they're in a vehicle, which side did the seller approach? Could you see who handed the money to the seller? Get descriptions and number of occupants out over the air. Keep in mind drug-rips happen all the time. Buyers are just as likely to have weapons on them as sellers are. So if your team pulls over a vehicle that's loaded down you probably should have at least two cars available. And nobody should be stopping a vehicle by themselves. That's why it's called an arrest team. Team meaning more than one person! We always worked with a partner and everything was always done in twos.

So now that you've got a couple good stops made and you found some dope, it's time to take down the seller. Make sure everyone knows that you're going after the seller now. Everybody should be moving in a bit closer and waiting for the word. After you observe the last sale, you have to articulate again who the seller is, his description and where the dope is at. Getting the seller secured is most important. After that, the take down team can then worry about where the dope is. Also, just so there is no confusion,

[51]

the officers doing the surveillance and observing where the dope is are responsible for the arrest. They are passing their information on to other officers who then are in turn making the physical arrest for them. The officers in the take down team do not have to see anything. They are going solely on what has been advised to them. The two doing the surveillance, remember, never leave their roost unless an officer safety issue arises, that way, once the cars come screeching up, you'll be able to keep eyes on the dope and see if it gets thrown down, handed off, shoved down the pants or shorts or whatever. After everyone involved is in custody, recovering the dope becomes paramount. No dope, no dope case and you're felony arrest will fizzle in to a misdemeanor and all that time and energy spent will be for not. To alleviate the above scenario, keep your eyes on the dope.

Utilizing K-9

If you have a K-9 available and they want to get in on the take down, by all means, let them. The bad guys would be ill advised to run but when the police come screeching up, their first reaction is to do just that. K-9's very rarely miss a running target so you're pretty much guaranteed not to lose the guy you're chasing. Plus it is great training for the dog and the handler so it's really a win-win for everyone except the bad guys.

When you're chasing after a bad guy that you know is running because he's been selling dope or got dope on him, you're going to use everything that you have at your disposal, including K-9, your taser, the fastest guys on your squad, your flashlight. It's about giving yourself the best possible odds for success that you can.

Recovering The Dope

Hopefully the guys that have had eyes on can direct you to exactly where the dope is. It's a lot easier obviously if they weren't keeping it on them and you can guide them right to it over the radio. But when the race is on it gets a lot trickier. Now you're relying on the take down team to watch that he doesn't throw it or destroy it somehow. We've already mentioned a number of hiding spots outside such as mailboxes and trees and bushes but when it comes to the bad guys hiding dope on their person, pretty much anything goes. Based on experience, bad guys like to hide dope where they think macho police won't go to look. As previously mentioned, this includes the crack of their ass and for a couple of different reasons. One, it actually does hold it and two; bad guys know most cops aren't going to be reaching into the crack of their ass to check for the dope (Unless you're a certain lieutenant, lmao! But that's a different story). When you have officers with eyes on, however, and they actually see a guy shoving a cherry flavored Chapstick container down the crack of his ass, someone's going to have to retrieve it. As eluded to earlier, just be prepared for them to start freaking out and yelling and screaming all kinds of obscenities at you. Just maintain your composure and professionalism because they're just trying to create a diversion. If it gets to the point where it's too much, then just call a supervisor and explain what you

[53]

have going on. More than likely he's just going to tell you to glove up! I would not throw him in the car though until you've recovered the dope. The exception to that would be if you could not see the dope at all. That would lead you to believe that maybe they've gone and fully inserted it which at that time you definitely would never strip the guy in the street. Always fully advise the jail nurse and more than likely it will unfortunately end with a trip to the hospital.

Where There's Dope, There's Money

In almost every case, if you have somebody standing out on the corner selling dope, he or she is going to have money on them somewhere. The only way I can see that not being the case is if the seller has passed off the money to owner of the dope. Your guys with eyes on should be able to pick that out as well and if nothing else, get a tag number or have someone follow the money regardless if they're on foot, bicycle or car.

If you've recovered the dope and they have money, seize the money as well; every time. If you were unable to recover the dope but they have a ton of money then there are a couple of things you can do. The first being; if you can articulate in your PCA how, based on your training and experience, the money was arranged in the bad guys pockets that is consistent with street level narcotic sales, i.e., the bills were all 10's or 20's and they were all folded over on top of each other, unlike bills in a wallet, then seize the money as well. You can also see if your department's K-9 unit will come over and alert on the money. If the dog does hit on the money, and depending on how your courts work, that would be an admissible link between the money and the sale of drugs.

When The Crowds Start To Gather

Inevitably, soon as the go is given and the apprehension phase is underway, crowds begin to gather. At this point you'll want to expedite things as much as you can. It's been mostly my experience that the crowds are not law enforcement friendly either, as you could imagine. In fact, you'll want to recover the dope as quick as you can and even put up a perimeter if you have to. Anybody that crosses the line gets arrested and charged with obstruction. There have been plenty of times when dope sellers suddenly switch hats and become all-star quarterbacks trying to get rid of their stash to anyone that will take it. Guns and cash can also disappear in a heartbeat if you're not watching everything that's going on. It's always best practice to have at least two officers posted up at the site of the arrest with their only responsibility being to watch the crowd. This leaves the others free to do their search and recovery work without having to worry about losing evidence or taking a bottle to the head. This is another reason why single officers should refrain from doing surveillance. Sure you can do the surveillance with no problem but you need to think about everything that is ultimately involved in such an operation.

CHAPTER 7

Transporting To Jail – Options

If you are so inclined, there are a few more options available than just taking your bad guy to jail. If you're already doing surveillance ops with your squad mates, then like I stated before, you guys aren't messing around and you're not afraid of a little work. That being said, with your new arrestee in tote, you'll now have the opportunity to try and develop a working relationship with him or her in the form of a confidential informant. Depending on who your bad guys are and believe me, you'll know who you can work with or not, this can be a win-win situation for the both of you. It will be immediately apparent for you but it's going to take a little longer for the bad guy to realize it's a win for them, as well. The way it works in many departments is this: you arrest a girl for selling dope and she starts freaking out. You have a little conversation about consequences then you tell her that there is a way that she can help herself out. She stops crying, the sun comes out and she wants to know how. So you tell her that there is a way that she can work the charges off by becoming a confidential informant. At first she'll be so excited because they all think that they're going to be magically unarrested right then and there. But it just does not work like that. The way it does work is that you get a solid contact number for the arrested person, you book them in just as normal and then you explain to them that if they want to help themselves out of their current situation then they need to call this number to speak to a detective. Now, of course you would have already had a conversation with one of your narcs and believe me, they love trying out new C.I.s. It's completely up to the bad guys or girls whether they want to call the detective (undercover narc) or not. Now, an exception to this is if you were to happen upon a situation where just arrested someone with a very large amount of dope or cash or guns or all three. It would then be up to your supervisor but they would probably become a person of interest pretty quickly and therefore warrant a detective being called in to talk to them. Most times, however, they'll just tell you to pass their number along and if they want to talk then they'll talk. It's no skin off our nose or the detective's nose at all and you still credit for the arrest. Most of the time, the arrested promise to get you AKs, Glocks, rocks, stolen cars, everything and anything under the sun and then do absolutely nothing, but at the end of the day guess what? Their charges still stick. If they do start working with you or narcs then a conversation with the State Attorney's Office is in order and together the State and the detectives will engage in how to proceed. Arrestees on probation that are looking at going back to prison for a while are good candidates but don't ever trust them. If your department does have a confidential informant program it should be closely regulated by General Orders and Standard Operating Procedures. Make sure you understand the in's and out of the program and never give a C.I. anything by yourself or even meet with a C.I. by yourself. Conversations over the phone are completely acceptable and happen all the time. In fact, most C.I.s will blow your phone up because they're always looking to get paid. Just make sure you know what your department's policy is when dealing with C.I.s so you can avoid getting jammed up.

CHAPTER 8

Writing The PCA

The two officers conducting the surveillance are going to be the ones responsible for writing the charging document and rightfully so, as they are the ones that actually have observed the hand to hand deal or deals. In describing the incident in the narrative portion of your pca, always use phrases like, "based on my experience and training", "hand to hand transactions" and things that are "consistent with street level sales of narcotics." Defense attorneys live to pick apart PCAs so put everything that you can in it or attached to it. This includes Google Earth print outs of where you were during the surveillance and where the bad guys were selling. Attach any previous patrol requests from concerned citizens and make sure anybody that had anything major or minor to do with the operation, such as helped with the arrest or helped find the dope, writes a detailed supplement to the case. And read everybody's supplement as well to make sure it's not coming from way out in left field. To put together a solid case, everyone needs to be on the same page. Everyone sees things a little bit differently, especially under stress. If you need clarification on someone's supplement, by all means, ask for it.

What To Charge: Enhanced Penalties

As mentioned earlier, if you're having an issue with street level drug sales within 1000 feet of a church, a park, a school or a day care or any other place that your jurisdiction deems worthy of enhancement, per state statute, make sure you tack that on to your charges. Usually it's just a matter of finding the right subsection that covers the enhancement. Not only does the enhancement add potential time to the suspect's sentence but if your case goes to trial, people, jurors, tend to get much more offended when somebody is selling dope 500 feet away from where children are attending daycare.

If you do charge someone with a particular enhancement, make sure you get with someone who has a laser and then shoot from where the bad guy was to where the enhancement is. And then put the exact footage along with the officer that took the measurement, the brand of the laser and the serial number of it as well.

CHAPTER 9

Prosecution Stage

Depositions

The most important thing I can say about depositions is not to miss them. Defense attorneys get all out of sorts and love to call the station to complain about officers missing their depos. Most times you only get a couple hours sleep if that before you're in there trying to remember what you did three months ago. One of the defense's tactics during the depo is to try and make you look as incompetent as possible. To alleviate this, do yourself a favor and get a copy of the report a couple days before your actual depo. Make sure you get the supplements as well. You don't want to mistakenly assume that another officer did something when they didn't, that just gives the defense extra ammunition to muddy the waters with.

Motions to Suppress

The only thing you really need to know about Motions to Suppress is that it's a tactic, plain and simple and usually two-folded. Defense attorneys love to call officers in on a Motion to Suppress because first and foremost, it delays the trial which is good for their client. Secondly it puts a lot more money in the attorney's pocket and lastly it has a way of shaking up officers in that it starts to make them second guess themselves and appear unsure if what they did was legal or not. That in itself then opens the door for alleged civil rights violations and so on down the line.

The way to resolve this issue is to do your homework before you're scheduled to appear at the motion. Get with the State and find out exactly what the defense is going to try and suppress. Regardless of whether or not it was a traffic stop, a search, consent issues, constructive possession issues... whatever the case is, as long as you discuss it with the State, you should be able to confidently defend yourself against any allegations of wrongdoing. Just remain calm and professional. Defense attorneys live to get officers all riled up. It's a game and just another tactic they use to get you flustered so they can misinterpret your words. And if you were with a partner, always make sure you both go over the case a couple times. When partners start telling conflicting stories that's when cases get dropped.

Courtroom Testimony

Testifying in court can be very intimidating. The only way to relieve that is by experience and preparedness. When you're up on the stand you want to keep your answers very short and concise. If you get all chatty-Kathy up there and get diarrhea of the mouth just because you're nervous, the defense is going to have a field day with you. Don't forget, they write everything you say down on their little pads and refer back to it during cross exam. And then, they refer back to your deposition that you took months and months ago and even years sometime. So don't just make stuff up as you go. If you're in a jury trial, the minute they think you're making stuff up is the very minute you lost the case. If you're not sure of something, always refer back to what you wrote in your reports and remember this as well: if you didn't write it, it didn't happen. So if you leave out anything in your initial report, for any reason, like it's late in your shift and you just want to go home or you're starving and you want to eat, you need to stop and think of the consequences of that.

The main thing to grasp about courtroom testimony is that it's the defense attorney's job to discredit the officer. Some defense attorneys are very good at it and love to make good officers look like despicable pieces of dog crap. It's up to you to expose the defense attorney's tactics to the jury so they can realize that, "Hey, this cop is professional and has remained that way though out the trial. I believe him." If you can do that, you'll start chalking up a bunch of marks in the win column.

CHAPTER 10

Keeping Narcotics Unit Updated

After each of the surveillance operations that you perform, it's always a good idea to write a short intel report on the case and send it up to your Narc Unit. Not only does it help them keep tabs on who's actually out there in the streets selling but it might hopefully provide a link to who is supplying and fronting the dope on the street.

There's a great deal of intel that can come out of each operation. From confidential informant cultivation to realizing there's a lot more of a demand for heroin or pills or spice on the streets that earlier thought. Or is weed and crack still king of the corner? With your name and ID# on the bottom of the reports, as we spoke about in earlier chapters, it's a great way to earn that very valuable respect from your peers and supervisors and State attorneys as well.

Afterword

If you take anything away from this book, I hope you can start to get out of your cars and start making some memories. Most importantly, however, officer safety must remain paramount. Make those first five to seven years the good times so you can have stories of your own to tell. Law Enforcement has changed a lot and continues to change every month. It's ultimately going to be up to you! Keep safe and keep putting the pressure on those bad guys!